The Secret of Switzerland's Economic Success

Emil Küng

Translated by Dr. Eric Schiff

American Enterprise Institute for Public Policy Research
Washington, D.C.

Emil Küng is professor of economics and social sciences in the University of St. Gall, Switzerland.

ISBN 0-8447-3321-0

Library of Congress Catalog Card No. 78-20276

AEI Studies 219

© 1978 by American Enterprise Institute for Public Policy Research, Washington, D.C. Permission to quote from or reproduce materials in this publication is granted when due acknowledgment is made.
The views expressed in the publications of the American Enterprise Institute are those of the authors and do not necessarily reflect the views of the staff, advisory panels, officers, or trustees of AEI.

Printed in the United States of America

CONTENTS

DEVELOPMENT OF EXCHANGE RATES	3
THE PRICE POLICY OF BUSINESS ENTERPRISES	4
THE BEHAVIOR OF TRADE UNIONS AND EMPLOYEES	6
HISTORICAL BACKGROUND	8

The Secret of Switzerland's Economic Success

The study of particular sectors of an economy shows that there are always enterprises successfully holding their own even when the sector to which they belong is unsuccessful. In other sectors, some firms make profits far above the average. Since the success or failure of some firms differs so significantly from that of others in the same group, we may well ask: What specific methods have the successful enterprises used that set them so distinctly apart from the others?

Such differences can also be observed in the performance of industrialized countries. Here, Switzerland presents the biggest puzzle. In fact, the Swiss traveller abroad finds himself again and again being asked: Why is not Switzerland plagued by stagflation as all other industrialized countries are? How has Switzerland overcome the dragon of inflation? Do you believe that so small and so export-intensive a country can stay permanently outside the circle of nations that suffer from currency debasement? And why is there full employment in Switzerland while in the surrounding economies we find large-scale and long-lasting unemployment?

This last question is the easiest one to tackle. The recent low level of officially recorded unemployment in Switzerland can be explained largely by the fact that many foreign workers have gone back to their home countries. In general, this outflow of foreign workers resulted from the workers' own decisions, rather than from outright dismissals by their employers. The impact of the outflow on the Swiss labor market was compounded by the fact that almost no new immigrants were allowed to enter.

In numerical terms, the situation can be presented as follows. The total number of employed persons (excluding the self-employed) was 3,114,000 at the peak of the boom in 1973. By 1976, the number had declined to 2,816,000, a decrease of roughly 300,000 or 9.57 percent. The decline included 185,000 foreign workers and 113,000 Swiss nationals. A substantial number of the latter were women who returned to households and workers who retired early with pensions. The level of unemployment would be well over 10 percent if the departed foreign workers were counted as unemployed.

It does not follow, however, that a liberalization of immigration policy would necessarily lead to higher unemployment. It would not be hard to find jobs for additional foreign workers. This raises issues, however, that cannot be further explored here. Suffice it to say that there are strong political objections to again increasing the share of foreign workers. These objections are partly based on ecological and economic grounds (for example, the fear of inflationary pressures emanating from expanded construction activity).

Switzerland was by no means spared the ravages of a major recent recession; in fact it was hard hit. Real gross national product declined by not less than 7 to 8 percent in 1975 and by another 1 to 2 percent in 1976. Only late in 1976 did real GNP begin to recover. But in 1977 GNP grew again rapidly, nominally by 4.4 percent and in real terms by 3.7 percent. During the recession, the country had to struggle with a cumulation of crisis factors—steep appreciation of the franc, severe structural difficulties in the building and watchmaking industries, and a general cyclical decline. Thus, even in Switzerland, elements of stagflation were by no means entirely absent. The rate of growth of the economy as a whole declined abruptly and quite substantially. In fact, during the world recession 1973–1975, the rate of decline of real GNP has been greater in Switzerland than in most other countries. It should be recalled that the GNP growth of the Swiss economy had been very rapid, in large part because of the influx of foreign workers. In 1973 foreign workers accounted for 30 percent of total employment and in 1975 the figure was still 25.6 percent, but in 1976 and 1977 the share of foreign workers declined to 23.7 and 22.5 percent respectively.

The question suggested by these observations, then, is:

How did Switzerland manage to cope with these setbacks without creating intolerable tensions? One more figure brings the difficulty of the task into sharp focus: in 1975 business profits declined by not less than 22 percent. The business firms accepted the challenge. They successfully concentrated on cost cutting, rationalization, and innovation, and results appeared in due course. For example, in 1977, business was able to raise exports by 10 to 15 percent. At the same time, workers accepted the changed economic climate without grumbling; they adjusted their wage demands to the new situation. The population at large realized that the expansion could not have continued indefinitely at the former rapid pace, based as it had been on the influx of foreign workers. So they acquiesced in the chillier economic weather conditions.

The most intriguing fact is that one small country was able to bring money erosion and the concomitant rise of the general price level under control, not merely for a short while but for a considerable time—more than three years now. The consumer price index has remained roughly level since the second quarter of 1975. This achievement is particularly striking in view of the fact that many of the conditions of Switzerland's success against inflation are also present in other countries. There, too, the central banks, which since the transition to floating exchange rates in 1973 have acquired the freedom to regulate the volume of money, are in a position to give price stabilization first priority among economic objectives.

Development of Exchange Rates

In considering Switzerland's peculiar position among industrial nations, we are struck first and foremost by the extraordinary appreciation of the Swiss currency. Nominally, the Swiss franc has appreciated by more than 100 percent vis-à-vis the dollar since 1970. The cheapening of foreign currencies has, at times, more than offset price increases on the world markets. For example, OPEC prices since the end of 1974 have changed little in dollars, but they have declined substantially in Swiss francs. Import prices expressed in Swiss francs declined in many cases. Clearly, these declines helped in the fight against inflation to a degree that can hardly be overestimated. It is equally obvious that the lowered prices of imports enormously intensified their competition with goods produced at home, forcing domestic producers to reduce their selling prices. Since imported raw materials, semi-finished goods, food, and investment goods cost less, there was a decline in the costs of materials and energy to industry, as well as to households, serving to dampen wage demands.

Given these conditions, the central bank was able to be more restrictive in its policy regarding the volume of money than central banks in other countries could be. It is hardly an exaggeration to say that Switzerland experienced a full-fledged stabilization crisis, one resulting not from the actions of the central bank, but from the coincidence of the worldwide recession with structural changes in some lines of production. At any rate, there is no doubt concerning the outcome: the inflationary mentality of the population has been eradicated more thoroughly in Switzerland than anywhere else. Prices, which had been expected to rise continuously, as they still are in most countries today, are now expected to remain flat or, in some cases, to turn downward. This is so unusual that further explanation is called for.

The Price Policy of Business Enterprises

For decades, the Keynesian assumption has been accepted widely that in modern times money wages cannot be reduced and that there is therefore little scope for downward price adjustment. We were supposed to be traveling on a one-way street, leading upward, with no turning back. Empirical investigations have often revealed an even darker picture. In some countries, when the steel industry or the automobile industry experienced a shrinkage in sales, it would *raise* prices. Underlying this reaction was this line of thought: with the reduction in capacity utilization caused by the decline in the sales volume, overhead costs had to be distributed over fewer units produced; consequently, unit costs went up, and to achieve some preset profit goal, sales prices had to be revised upward. The rules of the market economy postulate that prices normally rise in sellers' markets, where demand is strong and pressing. It was disturbing to discover the same reaction could also be elicited by a recession. It is largely due to this seemingly perverse behavior of supply prices that nowadays—in sharp contrast to the rule in times past—an erosion of the value of money cannot be stopped even by a sharp cyclical downturn of economic activity.

This is one aspect of the stagflation under which many industrial countries are still suffering. But the pricing policy of the overwhelming majority of Swiss business enterprises exhibits a different pattern. In many sectors of the economy, price levels could be observed falling below the levels of the preceding year. The intense competition of imports has contributed to these declines, in some cases depressing market prices to levels not high enough to recover all costs. A temporary decrease in costs and prices in the building trades was caused by the unprecedented contraction of that industry. Even so, it is remarkable that there are again many price declines.

Obviously, in Switzerland—contrary to what is true in many other countries—the market power of suppliers of goods and services is, normally, not very great, and it is hardly ever misused to obtain price boosts at the very time when demand slackens. Besides, suppliers are often faced by market power on the demand side, and the ability of buyers to push prices down increases substantially in periods of slack. The extent to which market power has shifted from producers to consumers in Switzerland is illustrated by the relationship between the manufacturers of brand-name products and the chain stores and supermarkets that sell them: the large-scale retailers have considerable control over the prices of the brand-name goods supplied by independent producers.

Certainly it is not unnatural for competition sometimes to become particularly intensive even in oligopolistic markets, but, according to the traditional view, price reductions should be rare exceptions in such markets. They do occur in Switzerland, however, even under oligopolistic conditions. Since it is natural for monopolies and cartels to resist price decreases, how have price declines become so common in a country that has often been considered to be one of the most thoroughly cartellized?

The answer is that the power of Swiss cartels and monopolies has been undermined to a decisive degree—largely as a consequence of two very important structural changes: first, and foremost, Switzerland has moved sharply in the direction of free trade. Generally low import duties were further whittled after Switzerland joined the European Free Trade Area (EFTA), which provides for duty-free entry of manufactured goods from other members of EFTA. In 1972 EFTA entered into an arrangement with the European Economic Community (EEC) for mutual liberalization of trade in manufactured goods. The second structural change that has undermined the market power of oligopolies and cartels is the rise of countervailing power of chain stores and supermarkets. As a result of these structural changes, prices in Switzerland have become flexible downward; we are no longer moving on a one-way street. The widely held view of downward rigidity of prices must be revised as far as Switzerland is concerned. Among the industrial countries this is certainly a remarkable phenomenon.

The Behavior of Trade Unions and Employees

According to the prevailing assumption, money wages are even more rigid downward than are prices. For several decades, money wages in industrial countries exhibited downward rigidity coupled with a high degree of contractually generated upward flexibility. The level of money wages gradually became tied to the rising consumer prices, thereby protecting an attained level of real wages, sometimes with legal underpinning. Over and above this, wage agreements sought to provide for increases in real wages in accordance with an expected rise in labor productivity.

What has been the picture in Switzerland during the last few years? In many recent instances, labor organizations have not pressed for automatic inflation adjustment of money wages. In part, to be sure, this new policy was facilitated by the very low level of the inflation rates. Moreover, workers were willing to forgo upward adjustments of real wages in line with productivity increases—adjustments that had come to be considered a matter of course. Thus, in 1977, productivity rose by about 4 percent, hourly earnings by 2.1 percent, and monthly earnings by 1.5 percent. As a result of all this, the proportion of wages in national income declined.

To understand this moderation in the attitude of labor, it is important to note that recently the share of business profits in national income has shrunk even more than wages. Profits have shrunk so much, in fact, that many firms had to draw on their reserves, and some even had to be liquidated or go into receivership. (What has gone up was the share of interest and rents.) The employees and their organizations had to face the question whether they, too, should shoulder some sacrifices or risk the economic breakdown of their employer. For the most part, they decided to regard job security as more important than anything else, including inflation adjustment of wages or participation in productivity gains. At least, this was the decision wherever the financial situation had been fully disclosed and communication between the "social partners" was reasonably well established.

The behavior of Swiss employees and their organizations showed a keen awareness of the constraints imposed by economic realities and actual market conditions—an awareness not found in the industrial relations of many other countries. Swiss employees and their organizations were willing to face losses; they demonstrated solidarity with their "class enemy," and, by so doing, they contributed to the maintenance of full employment. Another manifestation of this pragmatic mentality is the fact that Swiss trade unions seldom oppose technological innovations. Normally they cooperate in efforts to raise productivity. Even today there is, in general, no tendency to oppose rationalizations that cause some loss of jobs but help to preserve the competitive strength of the enterprises.

In an economy where labor cost per unit of output is stable or even declining, there is less incentive than in other countries to create unemployment by replacing labor with machines. In this respect, Switzerland is significantly different even from West Germany, and it is partly due to this difference that Switzerland has maintained full employment. In fact, at present the number of unfilled jobs exceeds the number of job seekers by a substantial margin.

There is no doubt that the willingness of labor to come to terms with the employers has made it much easier to eliminate the domestically generated inflation and to neutralize some of the disadvantages caused by the appreciation of the franc. For the foreign observer, however, the question remains: How could labor be induced to cooperate? Obviously, such willingness to cooperate requires a consensus about national goals not easily achieved in peacetime, when there is no threat from abroad.

Historical Background

To understand why cooperation rather than confrontation is the rule in Switzerland, and why strikes are rare exceptions, one has to go back into Swiss history to recall how in times long past the wars of religion were overcome, and how a multilingual and confessionally split population learned to resolve differences without violence and thus to coalesce gradually into a nation. In other words, the tradition of cooperation and compromise is not of recent origin.

As early as 1937, the machinery and watchmaking unions agreed not to resort to strikes as means for resolving industrial disputes, and this agreement was again renewed in June 1978. With similar agreements also concluded in other sectors, it was much easier for Swiss industry than for the industries of other countries to meet delivery deadlines, which greatly enhances Switzerland's competitive advantage.

Given these conditions, it is understandable that nobody thinks of prescribing ceilings for wage increases, or of abolishing free collective bargaining. The wage agreements now in effect are, after all, absolutely noninflationary: wage increases do not exceed productivity growth and some stay below it. The pressure of competition on an enterprise also affects the trade union. In general, union members display little inclination to drive things to extremes; after all, they have much more to lose than "their chains."[1] Attention has often been drawn to the fact that in Switzerland the number of saving-books issued by the banks exceeds the number of inhabitants, a reflection of a high propensity of the people to save and to make adequate provision for their future. Because inflation is now practically nonexistent in Switzerland, even small savers can expect a positive real return (interest) on their savings; in many other countries, how-

---

[1] "The proletarians have nothing to lose but their chains." *Manifesto of the Communist Party* by Karl Marx and Friedrich Engels, 1848. Authorized English translation, edited and annotated by Friedrich Engels (New York: International Publishers, 1932), p. 14.

ever, the savers' interest becomes negative when allowance is made for rising prices and taxes.

Some even more general factors may be emphasized. In a society oriented towards achievement, certain rules of conduct have become deeply rooted in the minds of the people. A willingness to work hard and to fulfill one's responsibilities is widespread. If it were not for such factors, it would be impossible to explain how a high standard of living could have been attained in a country that has practically no raw materials of its own.

Tensions between classes are probably mitigated to an appreciable degree by the considerable upward mobility in Swiss society, where the lower classes exhibit a will to move up the social ladder. There is hardly any proletarian class consciousness any more; in fact, labor has come a long way toward a bourgeois status. It is true that the rich sometimes display conspicuous and therefore irritating consumption, but this occurs far less often than, say, in some Latin countries. In Switzerland, even cabinet members ride the bus, and not only on exceptional occasions. It can be said without exaggeration that in Switzerland democracy is not only a form of government but a style of living.

Because of such background factors, the Swiss people have been extraordinarily successful in making the transition from hectic expansion to a temporary stagnation, with its attendant stabilization crisis, and then to renewed growth. Few would have expected the unavoidable disappointments to be weathered with so amazingly little disturbance. In the decades of stormy growth, real personal incomes had risen by several percentage points year after year, as had also been the case elsewhere. This created the expectation that things would continue in the same fashion in the future. Under the blows of cumulative economic shocks, it would not have been at all surprising for the struggle for redistribution of income and wealth to intensify, and for frustrations and aggressions to appear, leading to attempts to evade the difficulties by resorting to inflation. Actually, however, the nation stood the test magnificently. For some time there was hardly any further rise in real incomes; in some cases they even declined. But the people took this in stride, without any loud protests, and underwent a phase of learning in which the new conditions for economic survival were recognized and were accepted. The inflationary mentality disappeared. The stern monetary policy of the central bank met with general approval. Swiss voters in several referendums went even further and demanded that the fiscal authorities also keep within the boundaries of available means and restrict expenditures.[2]

Thus, there are several "secrets" underlying Switzerland's economic success. First and foremost is the unusual restraint that characterizes both the price policy of business and the wage policy of labor and its organizations. Of equal importance is the firm policy of monetary restraint pursued by the central bank, with the full backing of the federal government and the support of the public. Another important factor is the very sensible and considerate manner in which the entire population met the challenge it had to face. There was no split, no loss of consensus about vital matters, and no flight into the self-deception of currency debasement and inflation. In this way Switzerland was spared the fate of other nations that continue to suffer from stagflation and seem unable to find a way out of that painful dilemma.

---

[2]This is reminiscent of the taxpayers' revolt—Proposition 13—in California, June 1978.

WIDENER UNIVERSITY-WOLFGRAM LIBRARY
CIR   HC397.K8
The secret of Switzerland's economic suc

3 3182 00200 7208

HC
397 .K8   152344